A
Topical
Bible
Guide

Bob Phillips

HARVEST HOUSE PUBLISHERS

EUGENE, OREGON

Cover by Terry Dugan Design, Minneapolis, Minnesota

TOPICAL BIBLE GUIDE
Copyright © 2004 by Bob Phillips
Published by Harvest House Publishers
Eugene, Oregon 97402

ISBN 0-7369-1274-6

Printed in the United States of America

04   05   06   07   08   09 / VP-MS /   10   9   8   7   6   5   4   3   2   1

Topical Bible Guide

President John Quincy Adams said, "I speak as a man of the world to men of the world; and I say to you, Search the Scriptures! The Bible is the book of all others, to be read at all ages, and in all conditions of human life; not to be read once or twice or thrice through, and then laid aside, but to be read in small portions of one or two chapters every day, and never to be intermitted, unless by overruling necessity."

This *Topical Bible Guide* has been designed to help you search the Scriptures on a daily basis. It provides a quick reference on 100 popular topics in the Word of God. *Topical Bible Guide* will help direct you to over 1,000 important verses. You can use the Guide as:

- a daily devotional study
- a tool to assist you in counseling others
- a help in preparing talks, Sunday school lessons, and sermons

> *The Bible is God's chart for you to steer by, to keep you from the bottom of the sea, and to show you where the harbor is, and how to reach it without running on the rocks or bars.*

> **—Henry Ward Beecher**

> *In regard to this great book, I have but to say, it is the best gift God has given to man. All the good the Savior gave to the world was communicated through this book. But for it we could not know right from wrong.*

> **—Abraham Lincoln**

Anxiety and Worry

MATTHEW 6:30-34

So do not worry, saying, "What shall we eat?" or "What shall we drink?" or "What shall we wear?" For the pagans run after all these things, and your heavenly Father knows that you need them. But seek first his kingdom and his righteousness, and all these things will be given to you as well. Therefore do not worry about tomorrow, for tomorrow will worry about itself. Each day has enough trouble of its own.

PHILIPPIANS 4:5-7

Do not be anxious about anything, but in everything, by prayer and petition, with thanksgiving, present your requests to God. And the peace of God, which transcends all understanding, will guard your hearts and your minds in Christ Jesus.

PSALM 16:11; 37:1,7; 43:5
PROVERBS 16:7
ISAIAH 41:10
PHILIPPIANS 4:8-9,19
2 THESSALONIANS 3:3
1 PETER 5:7

Assurance of Salvation

JOHN 10:27-30

My sheep listen to my voice; I know them, and they follow me. I give them eternal life, and they shall never perish; no one can snatch them out of my hand. My Father, who has given them to me, is greater than all; no one can snatch them out of my Father's hand. I and the Father are one.

ROMANS 8:37-39

No, in all these things we are more than conquerors through him who loved us. For I am convinced that neither death nor life, neither angels nor demons, neither the present nor the future, nor any powers, neither height nor depth, nor anything else in all creation, will be able to separate us from the love of God that is in Christ Jesus our Lord.

MATTHEW 24:35
JOHN 5:24; 6:37; 20:31
ROMANS 8:16,31,35
HEBREWS 13:5
1 JOHN 5:11-13

Battle of Armageddon

REVELATION 16:16

Then they gathered the kings together to the place that in Hebrew is called Armageddon.

REVELATION 14:14-20

A.W. TOZER

"The Bible is not an end in itself, but a means to bring men to an intimate and satisfying knowledge of God, that they may enter into Him, that they may delight in His Presence, may taste and know the inner sweetness of the very God Himself in the core and center of their hearts."

Beatitudes

MATTHEW 5:3-10

Blessed are the poor in spirit,
  for theirs is the kingdom of heaven.

Blessed are those who mourn,
  for they will be comforted.

Blessed are the meek,
  for they will inherit the earth.

Blessed are those who hunger and thirst for
    righteousness,
  for they will be filled.

Blessed are the merciful,
  for they will be shown mercy.

Blessed are the pure in heart,
  for they will see God.

Blessed are the peacemakers,
  for they will be called sons of God.

Blessed are those who are persecuted because of
    righteousness,
  for theirs is the kingdom of heaven.

Bereavement and Loss

PSALM 23:4

Even though I walk
    through the valley of the shadow of death,
I will fear no evil,
    for you are with me;
your rod and your staff,
    they comfort me.

PSALM 119:50

My comfort in my suffering is this:
  Your promise preserves my life.

DEUTERONOMY 31:8
PSALM 23; 27:10

Bowl Judgments

REVELATION 16:1

Then I heard a loud voice from the temple saying to the seven angels, "Go, pour out the seven bowls of God's wrath on the earth."

REVELATION 16

Christian Fellowship

MATTHEW 18:20

For where two or three come together in my name, there am I with them.

HEBREWS 10:24-25

And let us consider how we may spur one another on toward love and good deeds. Let us not give up meeting together, as some are in the habit of doing, but let us encourage one another—and all the more as you see the Day approaching.

PSALM 122:1,9; 133:1
JOHN 13:34

ACTS 2:42,46
1 CORINTHIANS 1:9
1 JOHN 1:3,7

Christian's Armor

2 CORINTHIANS 10:3-5

For though we live in the world, we do not wage war as the world does. The weapons we fight with are not the weapons of the world. On the contrary, they have divine power to demolish strongholds. We demolish arguments and every pretension that sets itself up against the knowledge of God, and we take captive every thought to make it obedient to Christ.

EPHESIANS 6:11

Put on the full armor of God so that you can take your stand against the devil's schemes.

EPHESIANS 6:10-18

Comfort

MATTHEW 11:28-30

Come to me, all you who are weary and burdened, and I will give you rest. Take my yoke upon you and learn from me, for I am gentle and humble in heart, and you will find rest for your souls. For my yoke is easy and my burden is light.

JOHN 14:1

Do not let your hearts be troubled. Trust in God; trust also in me.

PSALM 23
LAMENTATIONS 3:21-26
MATTHEW 5:4
JOHN 14:16-18
ROMANS 15:4
2 CORINTHIANS 1:3-5
2 THESSALONIANS 2:16-17

Confidence

PHILIPPIANS 1:6

Being confident of this, that he who began a good work in you will carry it on to completion until the day of Christ Jesus.

HEBREWS 10:35

So do not throw away your confidence; it will be richly rewarded.

PSALM 27:3
PROVERBS 3:26; 14:26
ISAIAH 30:15
GALATIANS 6:9
EPHESIANS 3:11-12
1 PETER 2:9

Crowns

2 TIMOTHY 4:7-8

Now there is in store for me the crown of righteousness, which the Lord, the righteous Judge, will award to me on that day—and not only to me, but also to all who have longed for his appearing.

JAMES 1:12

Blessed is the man who perseveres under trial, because when he has stood the test, he will receive the crown of life that God has promised to those who love him.

1 CORINTHIANS 9:25
1 THESSALONIANS 2:19-20
1 PETER 5:2-4
REVELATION 2:10

Danger

PSALM 32:7

You are my hiding place;
    you will protect me from trouble
    and surround me with songs of deliverance.

ISAIAH 43:2

When you pass through the waters,
    I will be with you;
and when you pass through the rivers,
    they will not sweep over you.
When you walk through the fire,

you will not be burned;
the flames will not set you ablaze.

PSALM 23:4; 34:7,17,19; 91:1-2,11; 121:1-8
ROMANS 14:8

Death

2 CORINTHIANS 5:6-9

Therefore we are always confident and know that as long as we are at home in the body we are away from the Lord. We live by faith, not by sight. We are confident, I say, and would prefer to be away from the body and at home with the Lord. So we make it our goal to please him, whether we are at home in the body or away from it.

PHILIPPIANS 1:21-22

For to me, to live is Christ and to die is gain.

PSALM 23:4; 116:15
ROMANS 14:8
2 CORINTHIANS 5:1
1 THESSALONIANS 5:9-10
2 TIMOTHY 4:7-8
HEBREWS 9:27
REVELATION 21:4

Deity of Christ

JOHN 1:1

In the beginning was the Word, and the Word was with God, and the Word was God.

JOHN 20:28

Thomas said to him, "My Lord and my God!"

MATTHEW 26:63-64
JOHN 1:1-14,18; 10:30; 14:9; 16:15; 17:10
ROMANS 9:5
COLOSSIANS 1:15-19; 2:9
TITUS 2:13
HEBREWS 1:3,8
1 JOHN 5:20

Difficulties

ROMANS 8:28

And we know that in all things God works for the good of those who love him, who have been called according to his purpose.

2 CORINTHIANS 4:16-18

Therefore we do not lose heart. Though outwardly we are wasting away, yet inwardly we are being renewed day by day. For our light and momentary troubles are achieving for us an eternal glory that far outweighs them all. So we fix our eyes not on what is seen, but on what is unseen. For what is seen is temporary, but what is unseen is eternal.

HEBREWS 5:8; 12:7,11
REVELATION 3:19

ABRAHAM LINCOLN

"I believe the Bible is the best gift God has ever given to man. All the good from the Savior of the world is communicated to us through this book."

Disappointment

PSALM 126:6

He who goes out weeping,
     carrying seed to sow,
will return with songs of joy,
     carrying sheaves with him.

JOHN 14:27

Peace I leave with you; my peace I give you. I do not give to you as the world gives. Do not let your hearts be troubled and do not be afraid.

PSALM 43:5; 55:22
2 CORINTHIANS 4:8-10

Discouragement

JOHN 16:33

I have told you these things, so that in me you may have peace. In this world you will have trouble. But take heart! I have overcome the world.

HEBREWS 4:16

Let us then approach the throne of grace with confidence, so that we may receive mercy and find grace to help us in our time of need.

JOSHUA 1:9
PSALM 27:14; 43:5
JOHN 14:1-3,27; 19:25-27
COLOSSIANS 1:5

1 PETER 1:3-9
1 JOHN 5:14
REVELATION 22:1-4

Divorce

MALACHI 2:16

"I hate divorce," says the LORD God of Israel, "and I hate a man's covering himself with violence as well as with his garment," says the LORD Almighty. So guard yourself in your spirit, and do not break faith.

MATTHEW 19:6

So they are no longer two, but one. Therefore what God has joined together, let man not separate.

DEUTERONOMY 24:1-4
MATTHEW 5:31-32; 19:3-12
MARK 10:2-12
LUKE 16:18
1 CORINTHIANS 7:10-15

Doubtful Things

ROMANS 14:19

Let us therefore make every effort to do what leads to peace and to mutual edification.

1 THESSALONIANS 5:22

Avoid every kind of evil.

ROMANS 14:1-23
1 CORINTHIANS 8:9,13
PHILIPPIANS 2:15
COLOSSIANS 3:2,5-10,17
TITUS 2:12-14
JAMES 4:4
1 JOHN 2:15-17

External Pressures

2 CORINTHIANS 12:9-10

But he said to me, "My grace is sufficient for you, for my power is made perfect in weakness." Therefore I will boast all the more gladly about my weaknesses, so that Christ's power may rest on me. That is why, for Christ's sake, I delight in weaknesses, in insults, in hardships, in persecutions, in difficulties. For when I am weak, then I am strong.

1 JOHN 5:4-5

For everyone born of God overcomes the world. This is the victory that has overcome the world, even our faith. Who is it that overcomes the world? Only he who believes that Jesus is the Son of God.

JOSHUA 1:9
PSALM 37:5
ROMANS 8:28
1 PETER 5:7

Faith

HEBREWS 11:1

Now faith is being sure of what we hope for and certain of what we do not see.

HEBREWS 11:6

And without faith it is impossible to please God, because anyone who comes to him must believe that he exists and that he rewards those who earnestly seek him.

ROMANS 4:3; 10:17
EPHESIANS 2:8-9
HEBREWS 12:2
JAMES 1:3-6
1 PETER 1:7

Fear

PSALM 27:1

The LORD is my light and my salvation—
　　whom shall I fear?
The LORD is the stronghold of my life—
　　of whom shall I be afraid?

PSALM 56:11

In God I trust; I will not be afraid.
　　What can man do to me?

PSALM 91:1-2; 121:1-8
PROVERBS 3:25; 29:25

ISAIAH 51:12
JOHN 14:27
ROMANS 8:28-29,31,35-39
PHILIPPIANS 4:19
2 TIMOTHY 1:7
1 JOHN 4:18
JUDE 24-25

Forgiveness of Sin

PSALM 103:1-3

Praise the LORD, O my soul;
    all my inmost being, praise his holy name.
Praise the LORD, O my soul,
    and forget not all his benefits—
who forgives all your sins
    and heals all your diseases.

1 JOHN 1:9

If we confess our sins, he is faithful and just and will forgive
us our sins and purify us from all unrighteousness.

PSALM 32:5; 51; 103:12
PROVERBS 28:13
ISAIAH 1:18; 55:7
JAMES 5:15-16

GEORGE WASHINGTON
"It is impossible to rightly govern the world
without God and the Bible."

Forgiving Others

MATTHEW 6:14-15

For if you forgive men when they sin against you, your heavenly Father will also forgive you. But if you do not forgive men their sins, your Father will not forgive your sins.

EPHESIANS 4:31-32

Be kind and compassionate to one another, forgiving each other, just as in Christ God forgave you.

PROVERBS 18:19
MATTHEW 5:44-47; 6:12; 18:15-25
MARK 11:25-26
LUKE 17:3-4
COLOSSIANS 3:13

Friends and Friendliness

PROVERBS 18:24

A man of many companions may come to ruin,
    but there is a friend who sticks closer than a brother.

JOHN 13:35

By this all men will know that you are my disciples, if you love one another.

JOHN 15:13-14
GALATIANS 6:1,10

Fruit of the Spirit

GALATIANS 5:22-23

But the fruit of the Spirit is love, joy, peace, patience, kindness, goodness, faithfulness, gentleness and self-control. Against such things there is no law.

Generosity

LUKE 6:38

Give, and it will be given to you. A good measure, pressed down, shaken together and running over, will be poured into your lap. For with the measure you use, it will be measured to you.

2 CORINTHIANS 9:6-7

Remember this: Whoever sows sparingly will also reap sparingly, and whoever sows generously will also reap generously. Each man should give what he has decided in his heart to give, not reluctantly or under compulsion, for God loves a cheerful giver.

1 CHRONICLES 29:9
PSALM 37:21
PROVERBS 3:9-10
MATTHEW 5:42

God's Care

PSALM 91:1-2

He who dwells in the shelter of the Most High
will rest in the shadow of the Almighty.
I will say of the LORD, "He is my refuge

and my fortress,
my God, in whom I trust."

1 PETER 5:7

Cast all your anxiety on him because he cares for you.

PSALM 31:19-20; 34:17-19
NAHUM 1:7
EPHESIANS 3:20
PHILIPPIANS 4:19
1 JOHN 4:16
JUDE 24

Golden Rule

LUKE 6:31

Do to others as you would have them do to you.

MATTHEW 7:12

Great White Throne

REVELATION 20:11

Then I saw a great white throne and him who was seated on it. Earth and sky fled from his presence, and there was no place for them.

REVELATION 20:11-15

Growing Spiritually

EPHESIANS 4:15

Instead, speaking the truth in love, we will in all things grow up into him who is the Head, that is, Christ.

2 PETER 3:18

But grow in the grace and knowledge of our Lord and Savior Jesus Christ. To him be glory both now and forever! Amen.

EPHESIANS 3:17-19
COLOSSIANS 1:9-11; 3:16
1 TIMOTHY 4:15
2 TIMOTHY 2:15
1 PETER 2:2
2 PETER 1:5-8

Guidance

PSALM 32:8

I will instruct you and teach you in the way you should go;
I will counsel you and watch over you.

ISAIAH 30:21

Whether you turn to the right or to the left, your ears will hear a voice behind you, saying, "This is the way; walk in it."

ISAIAH 58:11
LUKE 1:79
JOHN 16:13

Guilt

ROMANS 8:1-2

Therefore, there is now no condemnation for those who are in Christ Jesus, because through Christ Jesus the law of the Spirit of life set me free from the law of sin and death.

2 CORINTHIANS 5:21

God made him who had no sin to be sin for us, so that in him we might become the righteousness of God.

PSALM 32:1-2
EPHESIANS 1:7
COLOSSIANS 2:9-17
TITUS 3:5

Hell

MATTHEW 18:8-9

If your hand or your foot causes you to sin cut it off and throw it away. It is better for you to enter life maimed or crippled than to have two hands or two feet and be thrown into eternal fire. And if your eye causes you to sin, gouge it out and throw it away. It is better for you to enter life with one eye than to have two eyes and be thrown into the fire of hell.

REVELATION 1:18

I am the Living One; I was dead, and behold I am alive for ever and ever! And I hold the keys of death and Hades.

MATTHEW 5:22; 13:42,50; 22:13; 25:41,46
MARK 9:48
JUDE 7

Help and Care

2 CHRONICLES 16:9

For the eyes of the LORD range throughout the earth to strengthen those whose hearts are fully committed to him.

PSALM 55:22

Cast your cares on the LORD
    and he will sustain you;
    he will never let the righteous fall.

PSALM 34:7; 37:5,24; 91:4
ISAIAH 50:9; 54:17
HEBREWS 4:16; 13:5-6
1 PETER 5:7

Holy Spirit

ACTS 2:38

Repent and be baptized, every one of you, in the name of Jesus Christ for the forgiveness of your sins. And you will receive the gift of the Holy Spirit.

EPHESIANS 5:18

Do not get drunk on wine, which leads to debauchery. Instead, be filled with the Spirit.

ACTS 5:3-4
1 CORINTHIANS 3:16; 6:19; 12:4-6
2 CORINTHIANS 13:14
1 PETER 1:2

Honesty

EPHESIANS 4:25

Therefore each of you must put off falsehood and speak truthfully to his neighbor, for we are all members of one body.

COLOSSIANS 3:9-10

Do not lie to each other, since you have taken off your old self with its practices and have put on the new self, which is being renewed in knowledge in the image of its Creator.

ROMANS 13:13
1 THESSALONIANS 4:11-12
HEBREWS 13:18
1 PETER 2:11-12

Humility

ROMANS 12:3

For by the grace given me I say to every one of you: Do not think of yourself more highly than you ought, but rather think of yourself with sober judgment, in accordance with the measure of faith God has given you.

PHILIPPIANS 2:3-4

Do nothing out of selfish ambition or vain conceit, but in humility consider others better than yourselves. Each of you should look not only to your own interests, but also to the interests of others.

PROVERBS 22:4
MICAH 6:8

ACTS 20:19
1 PETER 5:5-6

Husbands

EPHESIANS 5:25-28

Husbands, love your wives, just as Christ loved the church and gave himself up for her to make her holy, cleansing her by the washing with water through the word, and to present her to himself as a radiant church, without stain or wrinkle or any other blemish, but holy and blameless. In this same way, husbands ought to love their wives as their own bodies. He who loves his wife loves himself.

1 PETER 3:7

Husbands, in the same way be considerate as you live with your wives, and treat them with respect as the weaker partner and as heirs with you of the gracious gift of life, so that nothing will hinder your prayers.

GENESIS 18:19
PROVERBS 23:13-14
1 CORINTHIANS 7:3
EPHESIANS 6:4

Jesus—Savior of the World

JOHN 14:6

Jesus answered, "I am the way and the truth and the life. No one comes to the Father except through me."

ACTS 4:12

Salvation is found in no one else, for there is no other name under heaven given to men by which we must be saved.

MATTHEW 1:21
LUKE 19:10
JOHN 3:16
ROMANS 5:8
EPHESIANS 1:7
1 JOHN 5:12

Judgment Seat of Christ

ROMANS 14:10-12

You, then, why do you judge your brother? Or why do you look down on your brother? For we will all stand before God's judgment seat. It is written:

"'As surely as I live,' says the Lord,

'every knee will bow before me;

every tongue will confess to God.'"

So then, each of us will give an account of himself to God.

2 CORINTHIANS 5:10

For we must all appear before the judgment seat of Christ, that each one may receive what is due him for the things done while in the body, whether good or bad.

MATTHEW 6:2-4; 25:14-30
LUKE 19:11-27
1 CORINTHIANS 3:9-15
2 TIMOTHY 4:8

Kingdom Age

ISAIAH 11:6

The wolf will live with the lamb,
 the leopard will lie down with the goat,
the calf and the lion and the yearling together;
 and a little child will lead them.

ISAIAH 60:1-3

Arise, shine, for your light has come,
 and the glory of the LORD rises upon you.
See, darkness covers the earth
 and thick darkness is over the peoples,
but the LORD rises upon you
 and his glory appears over you.
Nations will come to your light,
 and kings to the brightness of your dawn.

ISAIAH 14:7-8; 25:8-9
REVELATION 20:1-6

Lake of Fire

REVELATION 20:14-15

Then death and Hades were thrown into the lake of fire. The lake of fire is the second death. If anyone's name was not found written in the book of life, he was thrown into the lake of fire.

NAPOLEON

"The Bible is no mere book, but a Living Creature,
 with a power that conquers all that oppose it."

Liberty

JOHN 8:32,36

Then you will know the truth, and the truth will set you free….So if the Son sets you free, you will be free indeed.

GALATIANS 5:13

You, my brothers, were called to be free. But do not use your freedom to indulge the sinful nature; rather, serve one another in love.

ROMANS 6:6-7,17-22; 7:6; 8:2; 14:1-23
1 CORINTHIANS 8:1-13
GALATIANS 2:21; 5:1
COLOSSIANS 3:17
1 TIMOTHY 4:4

Living the Christian Life

PSALM 119:9-11

How can a young man keep his way pure?
    By living according to your word.
I seek you with all my heart;
    do not let me stray from your commands.
I have hidden your word in my heart
    that I might not sin against you.

EPHESIANS 1:3

Praise be to the God and Father of our Lord Jesus Christ, who has blessed us in the heavenly realms with every spiritual blessing in Christ.

JOHN 15:7
2 CORINTHIANS 5:17
COLOSSIANS 2:6
1 PETER 2:2
1 JOHN 1:7

Loneliness

PSALM 68:6

God sets the lonely in families,
   he leads forth the prisoners with singing.

HEBREWS 13:5

Never will I leave you; never will I forsake you.

PSALM 23; 27:10; 91:11
ISAIAH 41:10
MATTHEW 28:20

Lord's Prayer

MATTHEW 6:9-13

Our Father in heaven,
hallowed be your name,
your kingdom come,
your will be done
   on earth as it is in heaven.
Give us today our daily bread.

Forgive us our debts,
   as we also have forgiven our debtors.
And lead us not into temptation,
but deliver us from the evil one.

Lord's Supper

MATTHEW 26:26-28

While they were eating, Jesus took bread, gave thanks and broke it, and gave it to his disciples, saying, "Take and eat; this is my body." Then he took the cup, gave thanks and offered it to them, saying, "Drink from it, all of you. This is my blood of the covenant, which is poured out for many for the forgiveness of sins."

MARK 14:22-24
LUKE 22:19-20
1 CORINTHIANS 11:17-34

Lordship

MATTHEW 7:21

Not everyone who says to me, "Lord, Lord," will enter the kingdom of heaven, but only he who does the will of my Father who is in heaven.

ROMANS 10:9-10

If you confess with your mouth, "Jesus is Lord," and believe in your heart that God raised him from the dead, you will be saved. For it is with your heart that you believe and are justified, and it is with your mouth that you confess and are saved.

LUKE 6:46
ROMANS 6:13-16; 12:1-2
1 CORINTHIANS 6:19-20
PHILIPPIANS 2:9-11

Love

ROMANS 5:8

But God demonstrates his own love for us in this: While we were still sinners, Christ died for us.

1 JOHN 4:10

This is love: not that we loved God, but that he loved us and sent his Son as an atoning sacrifice for our sins.

JOHN 6:16; 15:9-14
ROMANS 8:35-39
1 CORINTHIANS 13
1 JOHN 3:1

Man's Need of Salvation

ROMANS 3:23

For all have sinned and fall short of the glory of God.

ROMANS 6:23

For the wages of sin is death, but the gift of God is eternal life in Christ Jesus our Lord.

Isaiah 64:6
Romans 3:10-18; 5:12
Hebrews 9:27
1 John 2:13-17

Mark of the Beast

Revelation 13:16-18

He also forced everyone, small and great, rich and poor, free and slave, to receive a mark on his right hand or on his forehead, so that no one could buy or sell unless he had the mark, which is the name of the beast or the number of his name. This calls for wisdom. If anyone has insight, let him calculate the number of the beast, for it is man's number. His number is 666.

Marriage Supper of the Lamb

Revelation 19:7-9

"Let us rejoice and be glad
　　and give him glory!
For the wedding of the Lamb has come,
　　and his bride has made herself ready.
Fine linen, bright and clean,
　　was given her to wear."
(Fine linen stands for the righteous acts of the saints.)
Then the angel said to me, "Write: 'Blessed are those who are invited to the wedding supper of the Lamb!'" And he added, "These are the true words of God."

Robert E. Lee

"In all my perplexities and distresses,
the Bible has never failed to give me light and strength."

National Responsibilities

ROMANS 13:1

Everyone must submit himself to the governing authorities, for there is no authority except that which God has established. The authorities that exist have been established by God.

1 TIMOTHY 2:1-4

I urge, then, first of all, that requests, prayers, intercession and thanksgiving be made for everyone—for kings and all those in authority, that we may live peaceful and quiet lives in all godliness and holiness. This is good, and pleases God our Savior, who wants all men to be saved and to come to a knowledge of the truth.

PSALM 33:12
PROVERBS 14:34; 29:18
ROMANS 13:1-7
1 PETER 2:13-17

New Heaven and Earth

ISAIAH 65:17

Behold, I will create
    new heavens and a new earth.
The former things will not be remembered,
    nor will they come to mind.

REVELATION 21:1

Then I saw a new heaven and a new earth, for the first heaven and the first earth had passed away, and there was no longer any sea.

ISAIAH 65:17-25
REVELATION 21–22

Obedience

1 SAMUEL 15:22

Does the LORD delight in burnt offerings and sacrifices
      as much as in obeying the voice of the LORD?
To obey is better than sacrifice,
      and to heed is better than the fat of rams.

JOHN 14:21

Whoever has my commands and obeys them, he is the one who loves me. He who loves me will be loved by my Father, and I too will love him and show myself to him.

PSALM 111:10; 119:2
ECCLESIASTES 12:13
ISAIAH 1:19-20
MATTHEW 6:24
JOHN 14:15
ROMANS 6:16
2 CORINTHIANS 10:5
JAMES 2:10
1 JOHN 3:22

Occult

ISAIAH 8:19

When men tell you to consult mediums and spiritists, who whisper and mutter, should not a people inquire of their God? Why consult the dead on behalf of the living?

JAMES 4:7

Submit yourselves, then, to God. Resist the devil, and he will flee from you.

LEVITICUS 20:27
DEUTERONOMY 18:9-12
1 SAMUEL 28:7-12
2 KINGS 21:6
ISAIAH 19:3; 47:13-14
ACTS 19:18-20

Occupation

GENESIS 2:15

The LORD God took the man and put him in the Garden of Eden to work it and take care of it.

2 THESSALONIANS 3:10

For even when we were with you, we gave you this rule: "If a man will not work, he shall not eat."

PROVERBS 14:23
ECCLESIASTES 9:10
ROMANS 12:11-13
EPHESIANS 4:28

One Hundred Forty-Four Thousand

REVELATION 7:4

Then I heard the number of those who were sealed: 144,000 from all the tribes of Israel.

REVELATION 14:1,3

Then I looked, and there before me was the Lamb, standing on Mount Zion, and with him 144,000 who had his name and his Father's name written on their foreheads....And they sang a new song before the throne and before the four living creatures and the elders. No one could learn the song except the 144,000 who had been redeemed from the earth.

Overcoming Temptation

MATTHEW 26:41

Watch and pray so that you will not fall into temptation. The spirit is willing, but the body is weak.

1 CORINTHIANS 10:13

No temptation has seized you except what is common to man. And God is faithful; he will not let you be tempted beyond what you can bear. But when you are tempted, he will also provide a way out so that you can stand up under it.

ISAIAH 41:10
PHILIPPIANS 1:6
2 THESSALONIANS 3:3
JAMES 4:7
1 PETER 2:9

Paradise and Hades

LUKE 23:43

Jesus answered him, "I tell you the truth, today you will be with me in paradise."

LUKE 16:22-26

Parents and Children

EPHESIANS 6:1-4

Children, obey your parents in the Lord, for this is right. "Honor your father and mother"—which is the first commandment with a promise—"that it may go well with you and that you may enjoy long life on the earth." Fathers, do not exasperate your children; instead, bring them up in the training and instruction of the Lord.

EXODUS 20:12
PSALM 148:12-13
PROVERBS 1:8-9; 6:20-23; 23:22,26; 28:7
COLOSSIANS 3:20-21
1 TIMOTHY 4:12; 5:4

Peace

ISAIAH 26:3

You will keep in perfect peace
    him whose mind is steadfast,
    because he trusts in you.

PHILIPPIANS 4:6-7

Do not be anxious about anything, but in everything, by prayer and petition, with thanksgiving, present your requests to God. And the peace of God, which transcends all understanding, will guard your hearts and your minds in Christ Jesus.

JOHN 14:27; 16:33
ROMANS 5:1
PHILIPPIANS 4:4-9
COLOSSIANS 3:15

Persecution

MATTHEW 5:10

Blessed are those who are persecuted because of righteousness,
    for theirs is the kingdom of heaven.

1 PETER 2:20

But if you suffer for doing good and you endure it, this is commendable before God.

MATTHEW 10:22
ACTS 5:41; 9:16
ROMANS 8:17
2 TIMOTHY 3:12
HEBREWS 11:25
JAMES 1:2-4

DWIGHT L. MOODY
"I know the Bible is inspired because it inspires me."

Plan of Salvation

JOHN 1:12

Yet to all who received him, to those who believed in his name, he gave the right to become children of God.

ROMANS 10:9-10

If you confess with your mouth, "Jesus is Lord," and believe in your heart that God raised him from the dead, you will be saved. For it is with your heart that you believe and are justified, and it is with your mouth that you confess and are saved.

ISAIAH 55:7
JOHN 3:3; 5:24
ROMANS 10:13
EPHESIANS 2:8-9
TITUS 3:5-7
1 JOHN 5:11-13
REVELATION 3:20

Power over Satan

JAMES 4:7

Submit yourselves, then, to God. Resist the devil, and he will flee from you.

1 JOHN 4:4

You, dear children, are from God and have overcome them, because the one who is in you is greater than the one who is in the world.

Praise and Gratitude

PSALM 100:4

Enter his gates with thanksgiving
    and his courts with praise;
    give thanks to him and praise his name.

1 THESSALONIANS 5:18

Give thanks in all circumstances, for this is God's will for you in Christ Jesus.

HEBREWS 13:15

Through Jesus, therefore, let us continually offer to God a sacrifice of praise—the fruit of lips that confess his name.

DEUTERONOMY 8:10
1 SAMUEL 12:24
2 CHRONICLES 20
PSALM 34:1-4; 50:23; 51:15; 63:2-7;
107:8; 139:14; 147:1; 150
EPHESIANS 5:18-20
PHILIPPIANS 4:4-6
COLOSSIANS 3:15-17
HEBREWS 13:15
1 PETER 1:6-9

Prayer

MATTHEW 7:7

Ask and it will be given to you; seek and you will find; knock and the door will be opened to you. For everyone who asks receives; he who seeks finds; and to him who knocks, the door will be opened.

JOHN 15:7

If you remain in me and my words remain in you, ask whatever you wish, and it will be given you.

PSALM 10:17; 18:3; 86:5,7; 145:18
JEREMIAH 33:3
JOEL 2:32
MATTHEW 21:22
JOHN 14:13-14
ROMANS 10:9-13
EPHESIANS 6:18
HEBREWS 4:14-16
JAMES 5:16
1 JOHN 5:14-15

Provision

PSALM 34:10

The lions may grow weak and hungry,
    but those who seek the LORD lack no good thing.

MATTHEW 6:33

But seek first his kingdom and his righteousness, and all these things will be given to you as well.

PSALM 23; 37:3-4; 84:11
ISAIAH 58:11
2 CORINTHIANS 9:8
EPHESIANS 3:20

1 PETER 1:3-5
2 PETER 1:3-4

Purity

PSALM 119:9

How can a young man keep his way pure?
  By living according to your word.

1 JOHN 3:3

Everyone who has this hope in him purifies himself, just as he is pure.

PHILIPPIANS 2:14-15
1 TIMOTHY 5:22
JAMES 3:17; 4:8

Rapture

1 CORINTHIANS 15:51-52

Listen, I tell you a mystery: We will not all sleep, but we will all be changed—in a flash, in the twinkling of an eye, at the last trumpet. For the trumpet will sound, the dead will be raised imperishable, and we will be changed.

1 THESSALONIANS 4:16-17

For the Lord himself will come down from heaven, with a loud command, with the voice of the archangel and with the trumpet call of God, and the dead in Christ will rise first. After that, we who are still alive and are left will be caught up together with them in the clouds to meet the Lord in the air. And so we will be with the Lord forever.

Return of Christ

ACTS 1:11

"Men of Galilee," they said, "why do you stand here looking into the sky? This same Jesus, who has been taken from you into heaven, will come back in the same way you have seen him go into heaven."

TITUS 2:13

While we wait for the blessed hope—the glorious appearing of our great God and Savior, Jesus Christ.

LUKE 21:34-36
1 THESSALONIANS 4:13-18
2 PETER 3:8-14
1 JOHN 3:2-3

Rewards

EPHESIANS 6:8

Because you know that the Lord will reward everyone for whatever good he does, whether he is slave or free.

REVELATION 22:12

Behold, I am coming soon! My reward is with me, and I will give to everyone according to what he has done.

1 CORINTHIANS 3:11-15
EPHESIANS 5:27
2 THESSALONIANS 2:14
2 TIMOTHY 4:8

1 JOHN 3:1-2
JUDE 24

Satan

JAMES 4:7

Submit yourselves, then, to God. Resist the devil, and he will flee from you.

1 JOHN 4:4

You, dear children, are from God and have overcome them, because the one who is in you is greater than the one who is in the world.

ISAIAH 14:12-15
EZEKIEL 28:12-19
1 PETER 5:8-9
2 PETER 2:9

Seal Judgments

REVELATION 5:9

And they sang a new song:
"You are worthy to take the scroll
    and to open its seals,
because you were slain,
    and with your blood you purchased men for God
    from every tribe and language and people and nation."

REVELATION 6:1–8:2

Self-Control

1 Corinthians 9:24-25

Do you not know that in a race all the runners run, but only one gets the prize? Run in such a way as to get the prize. Everyone who competes in the games goes into strict training. They do it to get a crown that will not last; but we do it to get a crown that will last forever.

2 Timothy 1:7

For God did not give us a spirit of timidity, but a spirit of power, of love and of self-discipline.

Proverbs 4:23-26
Romans 13:14
1 Corinthians 16:13
1 Timothy 6:11-12
2 Timothy 2:3-5

Self-Image

1 Samuel 16:7

But the LORD said to Samuel, "Do not consider his appearance or his height, for I have rejected him. The LORD does not look at the things man looks at. Man looks at the outward appearance, but the LORD looks at the heart."

2 Corinthians 3:4-6

Such confidence as this is ours through Christ before God. Not that we are competent in ourselves to claim anything for ourselves, but our competence comes from God. He has made us competent as ministers of a new covenant—not of the letter but of the Spirit; for the letter kills, but the Spirit gives life.

PSALM 138:8; 139:14-16
PHILIPPIANS 1:6
HEBREWS 12:2

Sex and Marriage

PROVERBS 5:18-19

May your fountain be blessed,
    and may you rejoice in the wife of your youth.
A loving doe, a graceful deer—
    may her breasts satisfy you always,
    may you ever be captivated by her love.

HEBREWS 13:4

Marriage should be honored by all, and the marriage bed kept pure, for God will judge the adulterer and all the sexually immoral.

SONG OF SOLOMON
1 CORINTHIANS 7
EPHESIANS 5:18–6:3
1 THESSALONIANS 4:1-7
1 PETER 3:1-9

Sickness

JAMES 5:13-16

Is any one of you in trouble? He should pray. Is anyone happy? Let him sing songs of praise. Is any one of you sick? He should call the elders of the church to pray over him and anoint him with oil in the name of the Lord. And the prayer offered in faith will make the sick person well; the Lord will raise him up. If he has sinned, he will be forgiven. Therefore confess your sins to each other and pray for each other so that you may be healed. The prayer of a righteous man is powerful and effective.

PSALM 41:3; 103:3
MATTHEW 4:23
JOHN 11:4

Signs of the Times

Physical Signs

MATTHEW 24:7-8

There will be famines and earthquakes in various places. All these are the beginning of birth pains.

LUKE 21:25

There will be signs in the sun, moon and stars. On the earth, nations will be in anguish and perplexity at the roaring and tossing of the sea.

ISAIAH 35:1-2
EZEKIEL 36:30; 38:14-16; 44:1-2
DANIEL 11:40; 12:4
MATTHEW 24:15
2 THESSALONIANS 2:4
JAMES 5:1-3
REVELATION 11:1-2

Social Signs

EZEKIEL 36:24

For I will take you out of the nations; I will gather you from all the countries and bring you back into your own land.

Matthew 24:6-7

You will hear of wars and rumors of wars, but see to it that you are not alarmed. Such things must happen, but the end is still to come. Nation will rise against nation, and kingdom against kingdom.

Genesis 6:5; 13:13; 19:4-5
Deuteronomy 28:63-67
Ezekiel 34:11-13; 38–39
Zechariah 12:2-3
Matthew 24:9-10,12,37-39
Mark 7:21,23
Luke 17:28-30; 21:24,25,29-33; 28:30
2 Timothy 3:1-5
Revelation 9:13-21; 21:8; 22:15

Religious Signs

Matthew 24:4-5

Watch out that no one deceives you. For many will come in my name, claiming, "I am the Christ," and will deceive many.

1 Timothy 4:1

The Spirit clearly says that in later times some will abandon the faith and follow deceiving spirits and things taught by demons.

Daniel 8:23-25; 11:36-45
Joel 2:28-29
Matthew 24:11,13-14,34
2 Thessalonians 2:4-8
2 Timothy 4:3-4
2 Peter 2:1-2; 3:3-4
1 John 5:19
Revelation 12:12; 13:1-8

Sin

ROMANS 6:23

For the wages of sin is death, but the gift of God is eternal life in Christ Jesus our Lord.

2 CORINTHIANS 5:21

God made him who had no sin to be sin for us, so that in him we might become the righteousness of God.

ISAIAH 53:5-6; 59:1-2
JOHN 8:34
ROMANS 3:23
GALATIANS 6:7-8

Social Responsibilities

MATTHEW 5:13-16

You are the salt of the earth. But if the salt loses its saltiness, how can it be made salty again? It is no longer good for anything, except to be thrown out and trampled by men.

You are the light of the world. A city on a hill cannot be hidden. Neither do people light a lamp and put it under a bowl. Instead they put it on its stand, and it gives light to everyone in the house. In the same way, let your light shine before men, that they may see your good deeds and praise your Father in heaven.

1 JOHN 3:17-18

If anyone has material possessions and sees his brother in need but has no pity on him, how can the love of God be in him? Dear children, let us not love with words or tongue but with actions and in truth.

PROVERBS 19:17
MATTHEW 10:42
LUKE 3:10-11
GALATIANS 6:1-5

Sorrow

MATTHEW 11:28-30

Come to me, all you who are weary and burdened, and I will give you rest. Take my yoke upon you and learn from me, for I am gentle and humble in heart, and you will find rest for your souls. For my yoke is easy and my burden is light.

2 CORINTHIANS 4:16-18

Therefore we do not lose heart. Though outwardly we are wasting away, yet inwardly we are being renewed day by day. For our light and momentary troubles are achieving for us an eternal glory that far outweighs them all. So we fix our eyes not on what is seen, but on what is unseen. For what is seen is temporary, but what is unseen is eternal.

JOB 5:17-18
PROVERBS 10:22
ISAIAH 53:4
JOHN 16:22
2 CORINTHIANS 1:3-5; 6:10
1 THESSALONIANS 4:13
1 PETER 1:7; 4:12-13
REVELATION 21:4

Spiritual Gifts

ROMANS 12:6-8

We have different gifts, according to the grace given us. If a man's gift is prophesying, let him use it in proportion to his faith. If it is serving, let him serve; if it is teaching, let him teach; if it is encouraging, let him encourage; if it is contributing to the needs of others, let him give generously; if it is leadership, let him govern diligently; if it is showing mercy, let him do it cheerfully.

1 CORINTHIANS 12:4-6

There are different kinds of gifts, but the same Spirit. There are different kinds of service, but the same Lord. There are different kinds of working, but the same God works all of them in all men.

1 CORINTHIANS 12–14
EPHESIANS 4:11-12
1 PETER 4:10

Strength

ISAIAH 40:29-31

He gives strength to the weary
　　and increases the power of the weak.
Even youths grow tired and weary,
　　and young men stumble and fall;
but those who hope in the LORD
　　will renew their strength.
They will soar on wings like eagles;
　　they will run and not grow weary,
　　they will walk and not be faint.

2 CORINTHIANS 12:8-10

But he said to me, "My grace is sufficient for you, for my power is made perfect in weakness." Therefore I will boast all the more gladly about my weaknesses, so that Christ's power may rest on me. That is why, for Christ's sake, I delight in weaknesses, in insults, in hardships, in persecutions, in difficulties. For when I am weak, then I am strong.

DEUTERONOMY 33:25
PSALM 27:14; 28:7
ISAIAH 41:10
PHILIPPIANS 4:13

Study

PSALM 119:18

Open my eyes that I may see
  wonderful things in your law.

2 TIMOTHY 2:15

Do your best to present yourself to God as one approved, a workman who does not need to be ashamed and who correctly handles the word of truth.

PSALM 19:7-11; 119:9,11
ACTS 20:32
2 TIMOTHY 3:15-17
HEBREWS 4:12
1 PETER 2:2

Suffering

ROMANS 8:18

I consider that our present sufferings are not worth comparing with the glory that will be revealed in us.

1 PETER 5:10

And the God of all grace, who called you to his eternal glory in Christ, after you have suffered a little while, will himself restore you and make you strong, firm and steadfast.

2 CORINTHIANS 1:5
PHILIPPIANS 1:29; 3:10
2 TIMOTHY 2:12
1 PETER 1:6-7; 2:19; 4:12-13,16

Temptation

1 CORINTHIANS 10:12-13

So, if you think you are standing firm, be careful that you don't fall! No temptation has seized you except what is common to man. And God is faithful; he will not let you be tempted beyond what you can bear. But when you are tempted, he will also provide a way out so that you can stand up under it.

HEBREWS 2:18

Because he himself suffered when he was tempted, he is able to help those who are being tempted.

PSALM 94:17-18
PROVERBS 28:13
MATTHEW 26:41

HEBREWS 4:14-16
JAMES 1:2-3,12,14; 4:7
1 PETER 1:6
2 PETER 2:9
1 JOHN 4:4
JUDE 24

Ten Commandments

EXODUS 20:1-17

I am the LORD your God, who brought you out of Egypt, out of the land of slavery.

You shall have no other gods before me.

You shall not make for yourself an idol in the form of anything in heaven above or on the earth beneath or in the waters below. You shall not bow down to them or worship them; for I, the LORD your God, am a jealous God, punishing the children for the sin of the fathers to the third and fourth generation of those who hate me, but showing love to a thousand [generations] of those who love me and keep my commandments.

You shall not misuse the name of the LORD your God, for the LORD will not hold anyone guiltless who misuses his name.

Remember the Sabbath day by keeping it holy. Six days you shall labor and do all your work, but the seventh day is a Sabbath to the LORD your God. On it you shall not do any work, neither you, nor your son or daughter, nor your manservant or maidservant, nor your animals, nor the alien within your gates. For in six days the LORD made the heavens and the earth, the sea, and all that is in them, but he rested on the seventh day. Therefore the LORD blessed the Sabbath day and made it holy.

Honor your father and your mother, so that you may live long
in the land the LORD your God is giving you.
You shall not murder.
You shall not commit adultery.
You shall not steal.
You shall not give false testimony against your neighbor.
You shall not covet your neighbor's house. You shall not covet
your neighbor's wife, or his manservant or maidservant, his
ox or donkey, or anything that belongs to your neighbor.

Those Who Haven't Heard

ROMANS 1:18-20

The wrath of God is being revealed from heaven against all
the godlessness and wickedness of men who suppress the truth
by their wickedness, since what may be known about God is plain
to them, because God has made it plain to them. For since the
creation of the world God's invisible qualities—his eternal power
and divine nature—have been clearly seen, being understood
from what has been made, so that men are without excuse.

JOHN 6:45; 12:32; 16:8
ROMANS 2:15,18

CHARLES HADDON SPURGEON
"Nobody ever outgrows Scripture;
the Book widens and deepens with our years."

Tribulation Period

MATTHEW 24:21

For then there will be great distress, unequaled from the beginning of the world until now—and never to be equaled again.

REVELATION 7:14

These are they who have come out of the great tribulation; they have washed their robes and made them white in the blood of the Lamb.

DANIEL 9:24-27
REVELATION 11:2-3; 13:5

Trumpet Judgments

REVELATION 8:2,6

And I saw the seven angels who stand before God, and to them were given seven trumpets....Then the seven angels who had the seven trumpets prepared to sound them.

REVELATION 8–9

Trust

PROVERBS 3:5-6

Trust in the LORD with all your heart
    and lean not on your own understanding;
in all your ways acknowledge him,
    and he will make your paths straight.

Isaiah 26:3-4

You will keep in perfect peace
    him whose mind is steadfast,
    because he trusts in you.
Trust in the Lord forever,
    for the Lord, the Lord, is the Rock eternal.

Psalm 5:11; 18:2; 37:5
Isaiah 12:2

Two Witnesses

Revelation 11:3

And I will give power to my two witnesses, and they will prophesy for 1,260 days, clothed in sackcloth.

Revelation 11:3-12

Unpardonable Sin

Luke 12:10

And everyone who speaks a word against the Son of Man will be forgiven, but anyone who blasphemes against the Holy Spirit will not be forgiven.

Hebrews 10:26-27

If we deliberately keep on sinning after we have received the knowledge of the truth, no sacrifice for sins is left, but only a fearful expectation of judgment and of raging fire that will consume the enemies of God.

MATTHEW 12:22-32
MARK 3:22-30
LUKE 11:14-23
1 JOHN 5:16-17

Victory

ROMANS 8:37

No, in all these things we are more than conquerors through him who loved us.

1 CORINTHIANS 15:57

But thanks be to God! He gives us the victory through our Lord Jesus Christ.

2 CHRONICLES 32:8
2 CORINTHIANS 2:14
2 TIMOTHY 2:19
1 JOHN 5:4
REVELATION 3:5; 21:7

Will of God

ROMANS 12:2

Do not conform any longer to the pattern of this world, but be transformed by the renewing of your mind. Then you will be able to test and approve what God's will is—his good, pleasing and perfect will.

EPHESIANS 5:17

Therefore do not be foolish, but understand what the Lord's will is.

PSALM 37:4; 91:1-2
PROVERBS 3:5-6; 4:26
ROMANS 14:5
GALATIANS 6:4
PHILIPPIANS 2:12-13
1 THESSALONIANS 4:3
1 PETER 3:17

Witnessing

MATTHEW 5:16

In the same way, let your light shine before men, that they may see your good deeds and praise your Father in heaven.

ACTS 1:8

But you will receive power when the Holy Spirit comes on you; and you will be my witnesses in Jerusalem, and in all Judea and Samaria, and to the ends of the earth.

1 PETER 3:15

But in your hearts set apart Christ as Lord. Always be prepared to give an answer to everyone who asks you to give the reason for the hope that you have. But do this with gentleness and respect.

PSALM 66:16
PROVERBS 11:30
MARK 5:19

LUKE 24:48
ROMANS 1:16
2 CORINTHIANS 5:18-20
1 PETER 4:11

Wives

PROVERBS 12:4

A wife of noble character is her husband's crown,
    but a disgraceful wife is like decay in his bones.

PROVERBS 31:10

A wife of noble character who can find?
    She is worth far more than rubies.

PROVERBS 11:6; 14:1; 22:6,15; 29:15; 31:10-31
1 TIMOTHY 3:11
TITUS 2:3-5
1 PETER 3:1-6

DANIEL WEBSTER

"If we abide by the principles taught in the Bible, our country will go on prospering and to prosper; but if we and our posterity neglect its instructions and authority, no man can tell how sudden a catastrophe may overwhelm us and bury all our glory in profound obscurity."

More Books You Can Believe In™
from Harvest House Publishers

The Complete Book of Bible Promises
Ron Rhodes

Bible promise books abound—but not like this one! Two hundred alphabetized categories of verses include explanatory headings, insights from the original languages, and deeply moving quotes from famous Christian authors and hymns.

Find It Fast in the Bible
Ron Rhodes

A quick reference that lives up to its name! With more than 400 topics and 8000-plus references, this comprehensive, topical guide provides one-line summaries of each verse. Perfect for research, discussions, and Bible studies.

How to Study Your Bible
Kay Arthur

In this systematic approach to Bible study, Kay presents an inductive method that includes key words, context studies, comparisons, topical studies, word meanings, and more to help readers interact with and understand God's Word.

The Daily Bible™
F. LaGard Smith

Featuring the NIV text in a chronological/historical arrangement, this Bible lets readers experience history while daily commentary helps them understand God's love and provision.